Contributing Author
Rabbi David J.B. Krisef

Managing Editor
Karen J. Goldfluss, M.S. Ed.

Contributing Editor
Nancy Hoffman

Editor-in-Chief
Sharon Coan, M.S. Ed.

Illustrator
Agnes S. Palinay

Cover Artist
Lesley Palmer

Art Coordinator
Kevin Barnes

Art Director
CJae Froshay

Imaging
James Edward Grace

Product Manager
Phil Garcia

Publishers
Rachelle Cracchiolo, M.S. Ed.
Mary Dupuy Smith, M.S. Ed.

EXPLORING WORLD BELIEFS
Judaism

Author

Gabriel Arquilevich

Teacher Created Materials, Inc.
6421 Industry Way
Westminster, CA 92683
www.teachercreated.com
ISBN-0-7439-3685-X

©2002 Teacher Created Materials, Inc.
Made in U.S.A.

Table of Contents

Introduction

Why Teach Religion?

If your students were asked what they know about Hinduism, Islam, Buddhism, Judaism, Sikhism, or Christianity, they would likely respond with an overwhelmingly limited amount of information. Although they are impacted almost daily with information related directly or indirectly to religious issues, they often know little about the religions themselves or the lives of the great spiritual leaders.

Why has the study of religion been neglected? In the early 1960s, the Supreme Court declared state-sponsored religious activities within the schools to be unconstitutional. However, the Court emphasized that learning about religion is essential. Despite the importance of religion in history and culture, most schools have traditionally kept a distance. Fortunately, this distance is being bridged.

As our world becomes more interdependent, there is a need for everyone to awaken to one another's spiritual heritage. To a great degree, the world has been shaped by religion. To teach history without religion is equivalent to teaching biology without reference to the human body. School boards across the nation now recognize this issue and have begun to advocate religious studies within the framework of history.

Religious studies foster tolerance. This is, perhaps, the most valuable lesson. Racism and stereotypes are born largely out of ignorance. How wonderful to give students the opportunity to listen to a Buddhist speak or to visit a synagogue and ask questions of a rabbi. These kinds of direct contacts are invaluable.

Meeting Standards

The National Council for the Social Studies (NCSS) developed curriculum standards in the mid 1990s. These standards have since become widely used in districts and states as they determine essential knowledge and skills acquisition for students. At least two of the ten themes that constitute the social studies framework standards address the study of institutions, cultures, and beliefs. Theme I (Culture), for example, asks students to consider how belief systems, including religion, impact culture. Theme V (Individuals, Groups, and Institutions) challenge students to study the ways in which institutions, religions, or otherwise, develop and how they influence (and are influenced by) individuals, groups, and cultures.

Within the NCSS framework, these themes are addressed for all students (early grades, middle grades, and high school). Therefore, support materials such as the books in this series, are important resources for teachers to use as they work toward meeting standards in the classroom.

The Semitic Religions

When we speak about the Semitic religions, we are referring to Judaism, Islam, and Christianity. The word *Semitic* describes the people who came from the Middle East and their languages. Arabs and Jews are both Semitic. Christianity is a Semitic religion because it originated in the Middle East.

Another feature Semitic religions share is monotheism. The prefix *mono* means one while *theism* means "belief in God or gods". So although these religions differ greatly, they each believe in only one God. Later, you will be reading about polytheism, or the belief in more than one God.

Look at the map below of the Middle East. The writings of the Hebrew Bible originated in the land between the Jordan River and the Mediterranean Sea. As you will see, both Judaism and Christianity are rooted in these writings. This area is now the modern state of Israel. Its capital, historic Jerusalem, is sacred to all three Semitic religions.

Now, find the cities of Mecca and Medina in the Arabian Peninsula. The prophet Muhammad was born in Mecca, now the world center of Islam. Every year, millions of Muslims, members of Islam, make pilgrimages to this sacred city. Medina is where Muhammad set up the first Muslim state. These cities are now part of Saudi Arabia.

About Date References

The abbreviations BCE, BC, AD, and CE are common terms used to reference time. (In this series, BCE and CE are used.) Some students may not be familiar with one or more of these terms. Use page 47 to introduce or review the abbreviations with students.

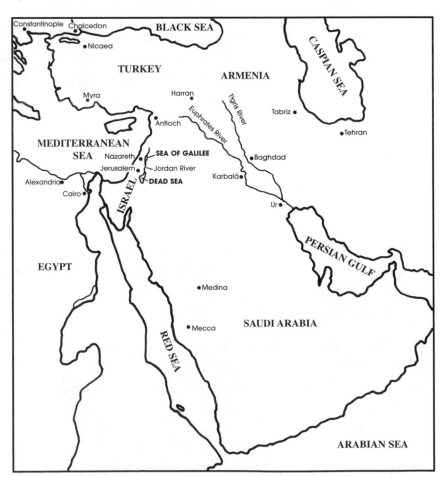

INTRODUCTION TO THE BIBLE

The Bible is the most famous book in all of history. It has sold more copies than any other book ever written. It has been translated into every major language in the world and can be found in nearly every hotel room.

The Jewish Bible was originally written in Hebrew, which is a very old language from the Middle East. Hebrew is written and read from right to left instead of from left to right as we read and write English. Another Jewish name for the Bible is Tanakh (kh is pronounced by rattling the back of your throat, like the German pronunciation of the composer Bach). Tanakh is a word created by taking the first letters of the Hebrew names for the three sections of the Hebrew Bible—Torah (the first five books); Nevee'eem (Prophets—books like Joshua, Samuel, Isaiah, Jeremiah, and Ezekiel); and Ketuvim (Writings, including books like Proverbs, Psalms, Esther, Ruth, and Lamentations).

The kind of Bible that you find most often in bookstores and hotel rooms is a Christian Bible. There are two differences between a Jewish Bible and a Christian Bible. First, the Christian Bible arranges the books from the Jewish Bible in a different order. Second, the Christian Bible contains 27 extra books that tell about the story of Jesus and the spread of Christianity, such as the Gospels and the book of Acts. These books were originally written in Greek, another very old language.

Sometimes, you hear Christians refer to the Jewish part of their Bible as the "Old Testament" and the Christian part as the "New Testament." Christians usually call the second part of the Bible the "New Testament" because they believe it has replaced the "Old Testament." Jews do not use these terms because they do not believe that the Tanakh has been replaced. Therefore, Jews and some Christians refer to the two parts of the Christian Bible as the "Hebrew Testament" and the "Greek Testament."

Citing the Bible

Before continuing, you should understand how to refer to chapters and lines of the Bible. When reading a quote from the Bible, you will notice it is followed by something like this: **Genesis 7:1-4**

What this means is that the quote comes from the book Genesis, chapter 7, verses 1 through 4. Try looking up this quote. Now, refer to the Bible to answer the following questions on the back of this paper.

Questions

1. What is the Torah? List the books it contains.

2. What is the difference between the Hebrew Testament and the Greek Testament?

 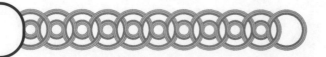

The Bible

READING FROM THE BIBLE: ADAM AND EVE AND THE GARDEN OF EDEN

There are many ideas about how the world began. One of the most famous creation stories is told in Genesis, the first book of the Torah. The word *Genesis* actually means *coming into existence.*

The following is the story of Adam and Eve and the Garden of Eden as taken from Genesis. If you have never read directly from the Bible, you may find it a little difficult. You will probably need to read it more than once and keep a list of vocabulary words. Note that the larger size numbers represent chapters and the smaller-size numbers are verses.

According to the Bible, God created the universe, including the heavens and earth, in six days. During this time, God created man from dust, breathing life into him. The Garden of Eden, or paradise, was also created. On the seventh day God rested. Our story begins at Genesis 2:15.

¹⁵ The Lord God took the man and put him in the garden of Eden to till and keep it. ¹⁶ And the Lord God commanded the man, saying, "You may eat of every tree in the garden; ¹⁷ but of the tree of the knowledge of good and evil you shall not eat, for in the day you eat of it you shall die."

¹⁸ Then the Lord God, said, "It is not good that man should be alone; I will make him a helper fit for him." ¹⁹ So out of the ground the Lord God formed every beast of the field and every bird of the air, and brought them to the man to see what he would call them; and whatever the man called every living creature, that was its name. ²⁰ The man gave names to all the cattle, and to the birds of the air, and to every beast of the fields; but for the man there was not found a helper fit for him. ²¹ So the Lord God caused a deep sleep to fall upon the man, and while he slept took one of his ribs and closed up its place with flesh; ²² and the rib which the Lord God had taken from the man he made into a woman and brought her to the man. ²³ Then the man said,

> *"This at last is bone of my bones*
> *and flesh of my flesh;*
> *she shall be called Woman,*
> *because she was taken out of Man."*

²⁴ Therefore a man leaves his father and mother and cleaves to his wife, and they become one flesh. ²⁵ And the man and his wife were both naked, and were not ashamed.

3

Now the serpent was more subtle than any other wild creature that the Lord God had made. He said to the woman, "Did God say, 'You shall not eat of any tree of the garden'?" ² And the woman said to the serpent, "We may eat of the fruit of the trees of the garden; ³ but God said, 'You shall not eat the fruit of the tree which is in the midst of the garden, neither shall you touch it, lest you die.'" ⁴ But the serpent said to the woman, "You will not die. ⁵ For God knows that when you eat of it your eyes will be opened, and you will be like God, knowing good and evil." ⁶ So when the woman saw that the tree was good for food, and that it was a delight to the eyes, and that the tree was to be desired to make one wise, she took of its fruit and ate; and she also gave some to her husband, and he ate. ⁷ Then the eyes of both were opened and they knew that they were naked; and they sewed fig leaves together and made themselves aprons.

READING FROM THE BIBLE: ADAM AND EVE AND THE GARDEN OF EDEN (cont.)

[8] *And they heard the sound of the Lord God walking in the garden in the cool of the day, and the man and his wife hid themselves from the presence of the Lord God among the trees of the garden.* [9] *But the Lord God called to the man, and said to him, "Where are you?"* [10] *And he said, "I heard the sound of thee in the garden and I was afraid because I was naked; and I hid myself."* [11] *He said, "Who told you that you were naked? Have you eaten of the tree which I commanded you not to eat?"* [12] *The man said, "The woman whom thou gavest to be with me, she gave me fruit of the tree, and I ate."* [13] *Then the Lord God said to the woman, "What is this that you have done?" The woman said, "The serpent beguiled me, and I ate."*

[14] *The Lord God said to the serpent,*
> *"Because you have done this,*
> *cursed are you above all cattle,*
> *and above all wild animals;*
> *upon your belly you shall go,*
> *and dust you shall eat all*
> *the days of your life.*
[15] *I will put enmity*
> *between you and the woman,*
> *and between your seed and her seed;*
> *he shall bruise your head,*
> *and you shall bruise his heel."*

[16] *To the woman he said,*
> *"I will greatly multiply your pain in childbearing;*
> *in pain you shall bring forth children,*
> *yet your desire shall be for your husband,*
> *and he shall rule over you."*

[17] *And to Adam he said,*
> *"Because you have listened to the voice of your wife,*
> *and have eaten of the tree of which I commanded you,*
> *'you shall not eat of it,'*
> *cursed is the ground because of you;*
> *in toil you shall eat of it*
> *all the days of your life;*
[18] *thorns and thistles it shall bring forth to you;*
> *and you shall eat the plants of the field.*
[19] *In the sweat of your face*
> *you shall eat bread*
> *until you return to the ground,*
> *for out of it you were taken;*
> *you are dust,*
> *and to dust you shall return."*

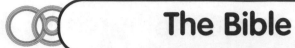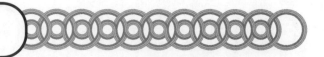
READING FROM THE BIBLE: ADAM AND EVE AND THE GARDEN OF EDEN (cont.)

20 The man called his wife's name Eve, because she was the mother of all living. 21 And the Lord God made for Adam and for his wife garments of skins, and clothed them.

22 Then the Lord God said, "Behold, the man has become like one of us, knowing good and evil; he must not be allowed to reach out his hand and take also from the tree of life and eat, and live forever."

23 So the Lord God sent him forth from the Garden of Eden, to till the ground from which he was taken.

24 He drove out the man; and at the east of the garden of Eden he placed the cherubim, and a flaming sword which turned every way, to guard the way to the tree of life.

Questions

1. What is the one commandment God gives Adam in the Garden of Eden? _____
   _____

2. What is Adam's first job in the garden? _____

3. How is Eve created? _____

4. The serpent is called "subtle." What does this word mean? _____

5. Why do you think some people refer to the serpent as the "tempter"? _____

6. What finally convinces Eve to eat from the tree? _____

7. Describe what happens to Adam and Eve immediately after they eat the forbidden fruit. How do they feel? _____
   _____

8. In this story, God punishes. What are the punishments for the snakes, for Eve, and for Adam?
   _____
   _____
   _____
   _____
   _____
   _____

9. What reason does God give for casting Adam and Eve out of the garden? _____
   _____

Abraham the Patriarch

In order to understand the origins of Judaism, we must travel back almost 4000 years to the land of Ur. It was here that a boy named Abram was born. According to the Torah, God chose Abram to be the father of a great nation. Before the time of Abram, all people believed that there were many gods, such as a god of rain, a god of wind, a god of sun, and a god of the land. God made a *covenant*, or a sacred agreement, with Abram that he would worship only one God. As a sign of that covenant, Abram's name was changed to *Abraham*, meaning exalted father of a great nation.

When Abraham was young, his family moved north from Ur to the land of Haran. (Use a modern atlas and the map on page 10 to discover where Haran would be today.) It was in Haran in about 2000 B.C.E. that God made a covenant with Abraham. Abraham was about 75 years old when God said to him:

> "Go from your country and your kindred and your father's house to the land that I will show you. And I will make of you a great nation, and I will bless you, and make your name great, so that you will be a blessing."
>
> *(Genesis 12:1-3)*

So Abraham and his wife, Sarah, along with a small caravan, journeyed hundreds of miles to the land of Canaan. This is the place God had promised to Abraham. And though the land of Canaan has changed hands many times since Abraham's arrival, today it is the land of Israel, the Jewish homeland.

Sarah and Abraham grew old, but God granted them the miracle of a son, Isaac. In Genesis 22, God tests Abraham's faith by commanding him to sacrifice Isaac. Though Abraham's heart is breaking, he takes his son to the hills, binds him, and lays him on an altar of wood.

Abraham the Patriarch

As the old man reaches for the knife to slay his only son, an angel calls out to him, telling him to release Isaac.

> "Do not do anything to him. Now I know that you fear God, because you have not withheld me from your son, your only son." *(Genesis 22:12)*

The angel comes to Abraham a second time, assuring him that because of his faith he will have many descendants, and they will be blessed and prosperous.

Through these stories, it is easy to understand the importance of Abraham. You can read about all of the Jewish patriarchs and matriarchs in the book of Genesis. Interestingly, the Muslim religion also descends from Abraham's family. Before Isaac was born, Abraham had fathered a son with his maidservant Hagar. His name was Ishmael, and according to Jewish and Muslim tradition, he is the ancestor of the Arab people.

The Journey of Abraham

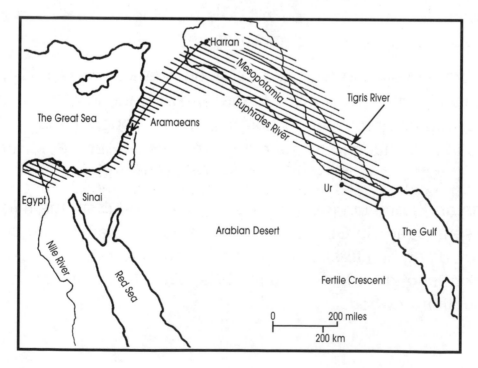

THE STORY OF MOSES

One of the most important chapters of Jewish history is told in Exodus, the second book of the Torah. It is the story of how God freed the Hebrews from slavery in Egypt and led them back to the land of Canaan. The word *exodus* actually means a mass departure.

As you will see, God chooses Moses to go before Pharoah, the king of the Egyptians, and demand freedom for the Hebrew slaves. After Moses leads the Hebrews out of Egypt, he takes them to Mount Sinai where they receive the Ten Commandments and the rest of the Torah. The Torah forms the bedrock of Judaism, containing detailed instructions on day-to-day living, rules by which Jews still live today. Thus, Moses is revered as the most significant Hebrew prophet, and the Exodus is the most significant event in Jewish history.

Many scholars think the Exodus took place around 1250 BCE. According to the traditional Biblical story, the Hebrews were enslaved in Egypt four hundred years before the "going out."

The Birth of Moses

Before the time of Moses' birth, Hebrew tribes had lived and prospered in Egypt. But the new Pharoah of Egypt felt threatened by the strength and influence of the Israelites.

Pharaoh ordered his soldiers to enslave the Hebrew people. He set cruel taskmasters over them. Without a moment's rest, the Hebrews were forced to build the store-cities of Pithom and Raamses.

THE STORY OF MOSES (cont.)

Although they were oppressed, the Israelites continued to multiply. They remained a proud and spirited people. The king of Egypt, sensing their resilience, grew determined and finally commanded his people to cast every newborn Hebrew son into the Nile. He allowed the daughters to live.

During this time, a son was born to a couple named Amram and Jochebed from the tribe of Levi. They hid the baby for three months and then placed him in a basket along the nile.

Then, Pharaoh's daughter, with her maidens beside her, came down to bathe at the river. She saw the basket in the reeds and sent her maid to fetch it. When she saw the crying child, the princess felt great pity and compassion.

"This is one of the Hebrews' children," she said.

Seeing this, the baby's sister, Miriam, came forward and asked if the princess would like a nurse to care for the child. She agreed, and so Miriam went to fetch her mother.

"Take this child," Pharoah's daughter said to Jochebed. "I will give you wages to nurse him for me." Unknowingly, the princess had asked the baby's own mother to raise him!

So the mother took her child and nursed him. The child grew and was brought to Pharoah's daughter and became her son. She named him Moses, which means *drawn out*, because she drew him out of the Nile. Moses grew up as an Egyptian prince in the luxury of Pharaoh's court.

THE STORY OF MOSES (cont.)

Moses in Midian

After Moses had grown up, he came upon an Egyptian taskmaster mercilessly whipping a Hebrew, one of his own people. Making certain none of Pharaoh's men were watching, Moses killed the Egyptian and hid his body in the sand.

The next day, Moses attempted to settle a dispute between two Hebrews who were arguing. When he asked one of them why he hit the other, the first responded, "Will you kill me as you killed the Egyptian?" Soon after, Pharoah learned of the murder and ordered the death of Moses. Fearing for his life, Moses escaped to the land of Midian.

Traveling one day, Moses came upon a well where seven women were filling troughs to water their father's flock. They were the daughters of the priest of Midian. When some shepherds tried to drive the women away, Moses protected them. After the priest heard of Moses' kindness he invited Moses to stay with them. Soon, Moses married Zipporah, one of the seven daughters. Together they had a son, Gershom, which means *a stranger there*. Moses chose that name because he, too, felt like "a stranger in a strange land."

In time, the king of Egypt died, but the oppression of the Israelites continued.

The Burning Bush

One day when Moses was tending his father-in-law's flock, he came to Mount Sinai deep in the desert. Suddenly, he saw a bush on fire. Strangely, though the bush burned, it was not being destroyed. When Moses came forward, God spoke to him from inside the bush.

THE STORY OF MOSES (cont.)

"I have seen the misery of my people who are in Egypt. I have come to deliver them out of that land, into a land flowing with milk and honey. Come now, I will send you to Pharaoh. Lead my people, the children of Israel, out of Egypt."

Moses wondered why he should be the one to free the Hebrews, but God reassured him. Then, God told him to gather the Hebrew elders and to beg Pharaoh to allow them three day's journey in the desert to worship the Lord God. Then God added,

"I know that the king of Egypt will not let you go, so I will stretch out my hand and strike Egypt with all my wonders. After that he will let you go."

"But they will not believe me," answered Moses.

Then, God asked Moses to cast his shepherd's rod to the ground. When he did, the rod became a snake. But when Moses retrieved the rod, it returned to its original form. Next, God had Moses place his hand to his breast. When he removed it, his hand was white and decayed like a leper's. Again he put his hand against his breast, and it became normal.

"If they believe neither of these signs," instructed the Lord, "pour water from the river on the land. The water will become blood."

Because Moses argued that he was "slow of speech and tongue," God told him that his brother, Aaron, would speak on his behalf.

Moses Returns to Egypt

And so Moses returned to Egypt. Moses and his brother, Aaron, went before Pharaoh and said to him, "These are the words of the God of Israel: 'Let my people go, so that they may hold a feast to me in the wilderness.'"

THE STORY OF MOSES (cont.)

But Pharaoh did not believe them and sent them away. His heart hardened, and that same day he gave these orders to the taskmakers: "No longer give the people straw to make bricks. Let them gather straw for themselves. But demand the same number of bricks they made before, for they have grown lazy."

After Pharaoh's command, the misery of the slaves was multiplied. Though they worked relentlessly, they could not make enough bricks. For this they were beaten and even killed. The Hebrews felt great resentment toward Moses and Aaron, for the brothers had made their plight even worse.

Moses returned to the Lord and asked him why his people had been treated so badly. Why had they not been saved? God assured Moses that the people of Israel would be freed and instructed him to return to Pharoah.

"Tell Pharaoh to send the children of Israel out of his land. Pharaoh will not listen, so I will perform many miracles and bring my people out of Egypt. And the Egyptians will know that I am the Lord."

The Ten Plagues

Moses was eighty years old and Aaron was eighty-three years old when they went before Pharaoh. Upon Gods instruction, Moses handed his shepherd's rod to Aaron. Aaron cast it on the ground, and the rod became a snake.

But Pharaoh was not impressed. He sent for his wise men and magicians who turned their rods into snakes. But Aaron's rod swallowed up all the others.

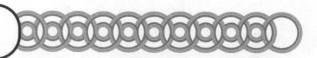
THE STORY OF MOSES (cont.)

Because Pharaoh would not listen, God told Moses to go out in the morning to the river Nile. There, in the presence of Pharaoh, Moses handed his rod to Aaron, who struck the water. The water turned to blood. The fish died, the river smelled foul, and the Egyptians could not drink the water.

Again, Pharaoh called upon his wise men and magicians. They, too, could turn the water to blood, so his heart remained unmoved.

Seven days later, God sent another plague. This time, when Aaron struck the river, thousands of frogs came from its banks. They swarmed over Egypt, entering every corner of every house and covering the land.

Seeing this, Pharaoh called upon Moses:

"Pray to the Lord to take the frogs from my people, and I will let your people go worship in the wilderness."

Moses prayed to God accordingly, and God answered his prayer. The frogs died. But when Pharoah saw the plague had ended, he changed his mind. He would not let the people go. So God sent a plague of lice to infest the animals and people. Yet Pharaoh remained unmoved.

The plague of flies came next. Swarms descended upon the land and the houses. Only this time, the land of Goshen, where the Hebrews lived, was untouched. Seeing this, Pharoah agreed to let the Hebrews go into the wilderness. Again Moses prayed that the plague be lifted and the flies disappeared. And once more, Pharaoh did not let the Hebrews go.

Even after witnessing the next plague—the death of all Egyptian cattle—Pharaoh would not budge.

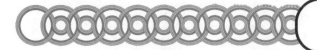

THE STORY OF MOSES (cont.)

The sixth punishment was the plague of sores. Sores appeared upon the bodies of all people and beasts of Egypt. Still, Pharoah did not set the captives free.

The next plague caused terrible hail, the worst ever in Egypt. Many witnessed the death of their livestock. Pharoah agreed he had sinned and promised to let the people go. But again, he broke his promise.

When swarms of locusts invaded households and fields, the same process took place. The ninth plague caused three days' darkness to fall upon Egypt; yet still Pharoah did not listen.

Although warned of the tenth plague, Pharaoh responded only with anger. All the firstborn in Egypt will die, Moses told him, including the firstborn cattle. But none of the children of Israel would die.

The Night of Passover

That night, Moses instructed his people to wipe lamb's blood upon the doorways of their houses. He told them to eat the lamb and be ready to depart thereafter. The Lord, Moses said, would not bring death to their houses. Seeing the lamb's blood, God would pass over their homes.

Pharoah woke that evening to the sounds of great cries. There was not a home in Egypt where someone was not dead. Even his own son died. Finally, after ten plagues, Pharoah set the Hebrews free.

That very night, after over four hundred years captivity, the Hebrew people journeyed on foot from Raameses to Succoth.

THE STORY OF MOSES (cont.)

Crossing the Sea of Reeds

God guided the Israelites as they traveled. By day, the Lord went before them in a pillar of cloud. By night, a pillar of fire protected them. But it was not long before Pharoah's anger rose against his former captives. He took his army and his best chariots to retrieve the Hebrews. Camping beside the Sea of Reeds, the Israelites saw the Egyptians marching upon them. Frightened and bitter, they asked their leader if they had escaped to the wilderness only to die. But Moses reassured them.

Moses turned in prayer to God, and God answered:

"Why do you cry to me? Tell your people to go forward. Lift up your rod and stretch out your hand over the sea, and divide it. And the children of Israel will go through the middle of the sea."

So Moses stretched out his hand and a strong wind blew all night. The sea divided, and the Israelites walked into the middle of it, a wall of water on either side.

The Egyptians followed, but God made the wheels of the chariots get stuck in the muddy sea bottom, slowing them down.

And when the Hebrews had crossed the Sea, God told Moses to stretch his hand over the waters again. As he did, the waters covered the pursuing Egyptians, drowning them all.

The Ten Commandments

For three months they traveled the desert. They passed through the wilderness of Shur, through Marah and Elim, the wilderness of Zin, and Rephidim. Though they were weary and the land was parched, God always provided. Finally, they came to Sinai and camped before the mountain.

THE STORY OF MOSES (cont.)

Moses went up Mt. Sinai to talk with the Lord. God told him to prepare his people for a special treasure. Moses told his followers to prepare themselves with prayer, that in three days the Lord would appear on the mountain.

When the third day came, a thick cloud with thunder and lightning lay on the mountain. A trumpet called so loudly that the people trembled. Moses led them to the foot of the mountain. Then, God called the prophet moses to the top and delivered to him the Ten Commandments:

"I am the Lord your God.

You shall have no other gods before me, you shall not make for yourself a graven image . . . you shall not bow down to them and worship them.

You shall not take the name of the Lord your God in vain.
Remember the Sabbath day, to keep it holy.
Honor your father and mother.
You shall not murder.
You shall not commit adultery.
You shall not steal.
You shall not bear false witness against your neighbor.
You shall not covet your neighbor's house . . . or anything else that belongs to your neighbor."

For forty days and forty nights, Moses stayed upon Mount Sinai listening to God's instructions. God told Moses laws regarding criminal behavior, destruction or theft of property, proper treatment of other people, and celebrating the Sabbath and other holidays. In addition, God instructed Moses to build a special Ark to carry the tablets of the Ten Commandments, and a holy sanctuary, called the *Tabernacle*, in which to house the Ark and make offerings of grain, fruit, and animal sacrifices to God.

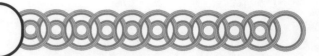

THE STORY OF MOSES (cont.)

The Making of the Golden Calf

Now, while Moses was upon the mountain, the people grew uneasy. Though they had been led out of Egypt and had witnessed miracles, they felt insecure without their leader. They turned to Aaron and begged him to make them a god so that they might not be alone.

Aaron told them to gather all their gold jewelry. Then, he melted it down and sculptured a golden calf and built an altar before it. The Israelites made offerings to the idol and celebrated.

Seeing this, God grew very angry.

"I will destroy them," God said to Moses, "and make a great nation of you alone."

But Moses pleaded with God not to destroy the Israelites, and God listened. Moses descended the mountain. He looked angrily upon the people who were dancing and singing before the golden calf. In fury, he hurled the stone tablets from his hands, and they broke at the foot of the mountain. Then he took the calf and burned it. He ground it into a powder, sprinkled it in water, and made the people drink it. The children of Israel mourned in shame.

Again, Moses climbed Mt. Sinai to ask forgiveness for the people. God granted them permission to continue their journey. God told him to make two more tablets of stone and return in the morning, and the words would again be written upon them. Moses did so and remained again forty days and nights. Though punishment came upon the guilty, God promised to have mercy and lead the Israelites into Canaan, driving out all the inhabitants of the land.

Exodus

THE STORY OF MOSES (cont.)

After forty years of traveling the desert wilderness, Moses finally delivered the children of Israel to the River Jordan, bordering the land of Canaan. Their entire journey can be seen on the map on page 22.

It was at the River Jordan, at one hundred and twenty years of age, that Moses completed his work. God told Moses he would not go into Canaan. After freeing the Hebrew slaves and leading them through the desert, it was time for him to die. He climbed Mt. Nebo, near Jericho, and God showed him the land the Israelites would inherit. The children of Israel wept for their great leader.

Questions

1. Why is this story called Exodus? Approximately when did it occur? _____

_____

2. Why did Pharaoh's daughter choose to call her adopted son Moses? _____

_____

3. Why do you think God chose Moses to be a prophet? _____

_____

4. List the ten plagues in order. Why was Pharaoh so stubborn about setting the captives free?

   a. _____   f. _____

   b. _____   g _____

   c. _____   h. _____

   d. _____   i. _____

   e. _____   j. _____

_____

_____

5. Why did the Hebrews make a golden calf? Which commandment does this break?

_____

_____

6. What two structures were used to house the Ten Commandments? _____

_____

TRADITIONAL ROUTE OF THE EXODUS

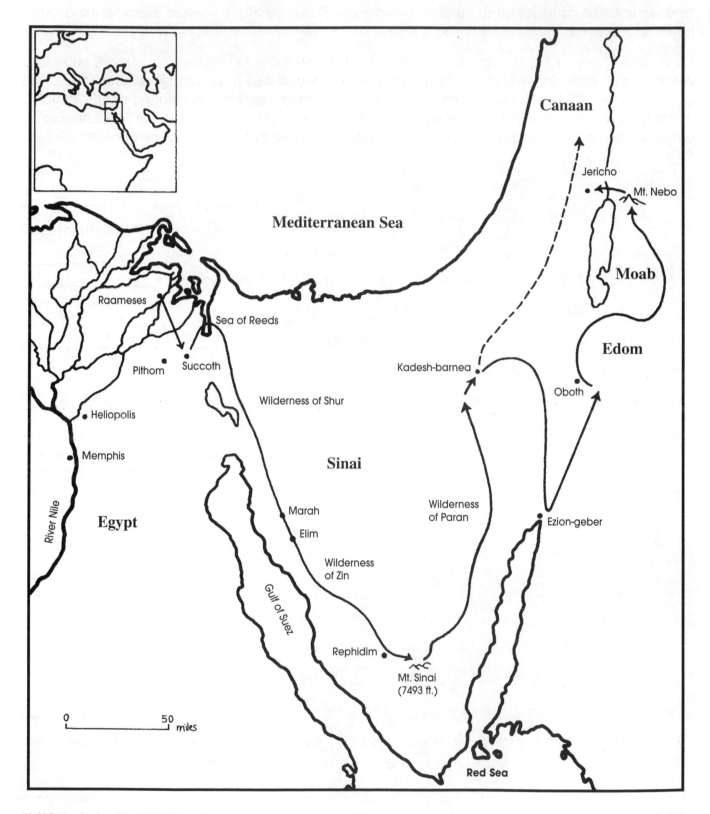

The Ten Commandments

Jews believe that God delivered the Torah to Moses along with 613 commandments! Some of them, such as commandments concerning animal sacrifices, no longer apply today. The most famous of those commandments are the Ten Commandments, which form an important part of Judaism and Christianity.

After reading each commandment, write down what you think it means. (For a more complete version, read from Exodus 20: 1-17.) Next, partner with a classmate to discuss the Ten Commandments. Are they reasonable? Why do you think each is a commandment? Which ones could you live by? Do you think these rules should apply only to Jews or to all people? Once the two of you have discussed your ideas together, share them with the class.

1. *I am the Lord your God.*

_____

2. *You shall have no other gods before me, you shall not make for yourself a graven image . . . you shall not bow down to them and worship them.*

_____

3. *You shall not take the name of the Lord your God in vain.*

_____

4. *Remember the Sabbath day, to keep it holy.*

_____

5. *Honor your father and mother.*

_____

6. *You shall not murder.*

_____

7. *You shall not commit adultery.*

_____

8. *You shall not steal.*

_____

9. *You shall not bear false witness against your neighbor.*

_____

10. *You shall not covet your neighbor's house . . . or anything else that belongs to your neighbor.*

_____

The Ten Commandments

Now that you have learned about the Ten Commandments, here is a chance to decide on some of your own. Remember to ask yourself if your commandments are really something you can live by.

 # The Ten Commandments

Use the lines provided to continue writing your commandments.

_____

_____

_____

_____

_____

_____

_____

_____

_____

_____

_____

_____

_____

_____

_____

_____

_____

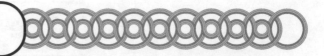

The Proverbs

Proverbs is the twentieth book of the Tanakh. Written by King Solomon around 960 BCE, this is a collection of sayings which contain pearls of wisdom to follow. The purpose of the book of Proverbs, according to Solomon, is the following:

For learning wisdom and instruction, for understanding words of insight;

For acquiring the discipline for success, righteousness, justice, and fairness.
(Proverbs 1:2-3)

Here are five proverbs from the Tanakh. Choose two of them and write what each one means to you. Then, write your own proverb and discuss it with a classmate.

1. "Happy is one who finds wisdom, and one who gets understanding, for the gain from it is better than the gain from silver and its profit better than gold." (Proverbs 3:13-14)

2. "One who seeks love overlooks faults, but one who harps on a matter alienates a friend." (Proverbs 17:9)

3. "A fool does not want to understand, but only to express an opinion." (Proverbs 18:2)

4. "A person's spirit can endure sickness, but low spirits—who can bear them?" (Proverbs 18:14)

5. "One who digs a pit will fall into it, and a stone will roll back upon the one who rolled it." (Proverbs 26:27)

A. _____

_____

_____

B. _____

_____

_____

C. _____

_____

_____

Respond

How can you apply these three proverbs to your daily life? Respond on the back of this paper.

WESTERN WALL

About 200 years after the Israelites entered the land of Canaan, in about 996 BCE, King David moved the Tabernacle and the Ark of the Covenant to Jerusalem and made it the capitol of his kingdom. David's son Solomon, the next King of Israel, built a magnificent Temple to replace the portable Tabernacle used while traveling through the wilderness. He chose to build it on Mount Zion, which some believe is the same mountain where Abraham was asked to sacrifice his son Isaac. Some of the largest stones that made up the wall around the Temple weigh as much as 40 tons and are still visible today! This Temple was destroyed in 586 BCE, when the Babylonians, led by King Nebuchadnezzar, captured Jerusalem and exiled the Jewish population to Babylonia.

In 516 BCE the Temple was rebuilt when the Jews returned from exile, and it remained in use until 70 CE, when the Romans captured Jerusalem and destroyed the Temple. The only part which remained was a portion of the external wall around the Temple mountain. This last remnant of the second Temple became the holiest of Jewish places. Before Israel gained control of Jerusalem in 1967, some referred to this wall as the "Wailing Wall" because Jews would go there to mourn the loss of the Temple. Since then, it has simply been called the Western Wall and has become a common place to visit. Many people write notes and leave them in the cracks of the wall, and some young people travel to Israel to celebrate a bar or bat mitzvah at the Wall.

Jerusalem has become one of the most famous cities in the world. Within the walls of the old city of Jerusalem are three of the world's most sacred religious sites. In addition to the Western Wall, there are Islam's Dome of the Rock, where the holy prophet Muhammad is believed to have ascended to heaven, and Christianity's Church of the Holy Sepulcher, where Jesus was crucified.

Extension

Chapter 6 and most of chapter 7 in the First Book of Kings contain detailed descriptions of King Solomon's Temple. Read these chapters and write a report on your findings.

Anti-Semitism

HOLOCAUST

Throughout history, Jews have suffered *anti-Semitism*, acts of violence and hatred against the Jewish people. Some of the worst incidents occurred during the Middle Ages, when Jews were accused of using the blood of Christian children to make Passover matzah. During the Crusades, Jews were massacred by Christians on their way to liberate the Holy Land from the Muslims, and in late 19th century Russia, Jews were victims of *pogroms*, organized attacks. But the most tragic and horrifying of all may be what happened in Germany prior to and during World War II, known as the *Shoah*, or the *Holocaust*.

Adolf Hitler, leader of the Nazis, blamed Germany's problems on the Jews and other minority groups. As his army swept through Europe, they attempted to eradicate the Jewish population, imprisoning and murdering millions. Jews were placed in concentration camps where they were systematically killed. In total, about six million Jews, out of a world population of 18 million, were murdered during the Holocaust. The map below shows the estimated deaths per country during the Holocaust.

Each year about a week after *Pesach*, Jews observe a special day called *Yom Hashoah*, Holocaust Remembrance Day, as a reminder of the horrifying consequences of hatred.

Minimum Estimated Deaths

4,600,000	Poland/USSR 1
402,000	Hungary 2
277,000	Czechoslovakia 3
125,000	Germany 4
106,000	Netherlands 5
83,000	France 6
65,000	Austria 7
65,000	Greece 8
60,000	Yugoslavia 9
40,000	Rumania 10
24,000	Belgium 11
152,000	Other countries

Beliefs and Observances

Monotheism

The most basic belief of Judaism is *monotheism*, the belief in one God. A *midrash*, a Jewish legend, teaches that Abraham's father was an idol-maker; and one day when Abraham was young, his father left him in charge of the store. Abraham took a wooden club and smashed every idol in the store except for the largest one; he placed the club in its hand. When his father returned and asked Abraham what had happened, Abraham told him that the idols got in a fight, and the largest one smashed all of the smaller ones! His father said, "Do you expect me to believe that an idol can do that? They are just wood and stone. Tell me what really happened!" Abraham responded, "If you really believe that idols are only stone and wood, why do you worship them?"

Chosen People

Another belief of Judaism is that the Jews are the "chosen people." This does not mean that Jews believe they are better than other people or that people must convert to Judaism in order to be loved by God. Rather, it means that God chose the Jewish people for the special responsibility of receiving the Torah and observing all of its commands and then passing the special ethical messages of the Torah to the rest of the world.

Messiah

Both Judaism and Christianity believe in a *Messiah*. The word Messiah is a Hebrew word which means "anointed." In Biblical times the coronation of a new king involved pouring a small amount of oil on his head, called *anointing*. Christians believe that Jesus was the Messiah (the name *Christ* comes from a Greek word meaning messiah) and that he will return. Christians also believe that the Messiah is the son of God. Jews believe that the Messiah will be a human being, a descendant of King David, who will bring the world to a time of complete peace in which every person will recognize and worship one God. Some Jews also believe that the Messiah will gather all Jews to the land of Israel, the Temple will be rebuilt, and there will be a resurrection of the dead.

Beliefs and Observances

Jewish observance is structured around doing *mitzvot* (commandments; singular, *mitzvah*). Mitzvot cover all areas of the life of a Jew, including religious obligations and other kinds of ethical behavior. Some examples of mitzvot follow.

Prayer

Jews are obligated to pray certain prayers three times a day—morning, afternoon, and evening. These prayers include the *Shema,* the most important statement of Jewish belief (see page 35 for two excerpts from the Shema) and the *Amidah*, a silent prayer in which they might ask God for certain things like health, wisdom, protection from enemies, and the coming of the Messiah. Some kinds of prayers are included only when praying with a *minyan* (10 people over the age of Bar or Bat Mitzvah; 10 men in Orthodox Judaism), so Jews are encouraged to pray with a community.

Tzedakah (charity)

Jews are obligated to give a certain percentage, generally at least 10–15% of their income, to tzedakah.

Kashrut (dietary laws)

According to the laws of kashrut, only split-hooved animals that chew their cud, certain types of fowl (like chicken, turkey, and duck), and fish with fins and scales are *kosher*—that is, proper to eat. Jews are also forbidden to mix dairy and meat products together at the same meal. In addition, animals (not fish) must be killed in a special way called *shechitah,* kosher slaughter, so they die with as little pain as possible. One of the purposes of the Kashrut laws is to sensitize Jews to proper treatment of animals.

Shabbat (The Sabbath)

On Shabbat, from sundown on Friday night until dark on Saturday night, Jews set aside time to rest. It is symbolic of God's seventh day of rest, after taking six days to create the world. On Friday nights and Saturday afternoons, Jews have special Shabbat meals, including blessings over wine and special braided egg breads called *challah.* In a traditional observance of Shabbat, Jews refrain from creative acts which change the state of the world, including cooking, shopping, lighting fires (including using electricity), sewing or knitting, and writing or coloring.

Reform Judaism

In the 19th century, the Reform movement changed significant parts of Judaism to make it more compatible with a changing world. For example, in the United States the language of prayer became English instead of Hebrew. In addition, Reform Jews believe that the mitzvot in the Torah are only meaningful if they add to one's relationship with God. Most of the traditional restrictions of Shabbat and Kashrut are not observed by Reform Jews.

Orthodox Judaism

In response to the changes that Reform Judaism was introducing, the Orthodox movement emerged. Orthodox Judaism asserted that every letter of the Torah was given to Moses on Mount Sinai, along with a detailed commentary. Therefore, all traditional practices of Judaism reflect the will of God and cannot be changed in any way.

Conservative Judaism

Conservative Judaism responded to Orthodoxy by saying that there has always been a way to change Jewish law and tradition, but the basic system of mitzvot cannot be changed. Most of the observances of Shabbat and Kashrut, for example, remain unchanged, although most Conservative Jews tend to treat them more liberally than do Orthodox Jews. Examples of changes include giving women an equal role in synagogue ritual (in most, but not all, Conservative synagogues) and more flexibility to change the traditional prayers to reflect modern concerns.

Reconstructionist Judaism

Founded in the mid-20th century, Reconstructionism is the most recent of the major movements of Judaism. It operates under the principle of "The tradition has a vote, not a veto." In other words, unlike Reform, the entire basic system of mitzvot is still an important part of Judaism; but unlike Conservative, an individual mitzvah can be modified or rejected if the community no longer finds it meaningful.

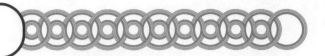

Rites of Passage

• • • • • • • • • • • • • • • • • Circumcision • • • • • • • • • • • • • • • • •

In the United States, it is very common for baby boys from many religions to be circumcised for medical or personal reasons several days after birth. For Jews, however, circumcision is called *Brit Milah*, "the covenant of circumcision." During circumcision, a piece of skin (called the foreskin) which covers the front of the penis is surgically removed. Curcumcision is done when the baby is eight days old, fulfilling the commandment God gave to Abraham in Genesis 17:10-13:

"Such shall be the covenant between Me and you and your offspring to follow which you shall keep: every male among you shall be circumcised. You shall be circumcised in the flesh of your foreskin, and that shall be the sign of the covenant between Me and you. And throughout the generations, every male among you shall be circumcised at the age of eight days."

There are also special ceremonies to welcome baby girls into the religion. Although there is no surgical procedure for girls, they are welcomed into the covenant with most of the same basic language as the Brit Milah ritual of the boys.

• • • • • • • • • • • Bar Mitzvah and Bat Mitzvah • • • • • • • • • • •

When a boy reaches the age of 13 years plus one day or when a girl reaches the age of 12 years plus one day, according to their birthdays on the Jewish calendar, they become *Bar Mitzvah* (for a boy) or *Bat Mitzvah* (for a girl). Literally, this means "son (or daughter) of the commandments." From that day on, they become responsible for observing all of the mitzvot (commandments) of Judaism. Prior to becoming bar or bat mitzvah, their parents were responsible for their religious behavior.

Preparing to celebrate a Bar and Bat Mitzvah in the synagogue requires years of study. The content of the synagogue celebration varies, but it commonly includes one or more of the following: reading from the Torah scroll, reading a selection from the prophets, leading a portion of the service, and delivering a speech called a *d'var Torah* (word of Torah) about the scriptural readings. In Orthodox synagogues, only boys celebrate Bar Mitzvah by taking part in the synagogue service. Following the conclusion of the service, family, friends, and the congregation join together for a festive meal.

• • • • • • • • • • • • • • • Marriage • • • • • • • • • • • • • • • • •

Marriage in the Jewish tradition is called *kiddushin*, which means sanctification. A wedding is a public ceremony in which the bride and groom commit themselves exclusively to each other. It is done publicly because the community is expected to help the couple live a life of loyalty and devotion to God and Jewish traditions.

Before the wedding ceremony, the bride and groom formally accept the provisions of the *ketubah*, the Jewish marriage contract which stipulates, among other things, that they agree to cherish, honor, and maintain each other (physically, emotionally, and spiritually) according

Marriage (cont.)

to the customs of Jewish marriage. The ketubah is then signed by two witnesses. Following the signing of the ketubah, the groom places a veil over his bride's face. The origins of the veil go back to the matriarch Rebekah, who, when she saw Isaac for the first time, "took her veil and covered her face." (Genesis 24:64, 65). The veil is symbolic of Jewish traditions of modesty.

The marriage takes place under a *chupah*, a wedding canopy representing the home that the bride and groom will create together. The rabbi recites blessings, the couple drinks wine and exchanges rings (in an Orthodox ceremony the groom does not receive a ring), and the rabbi recites seven special blessings comparing the couple to Adam and Eve, the two original human beings of creation. At the end of the ceremony, the groom breaks a glass, recalling the destruction of the Temple and reminding the couple that it is their responsibility to help fix the imperfect world in which they live.

Death

The Torah, at the beginning of Genesis, teaches us that human beings were created when God took a clod of earth, formed it into a human figure, and breathed life into it. When the breath of life leaves a body for the last time, Jewish tradition teaches that the body should be returned to the earth as quickly and naturally as possible.

For this reason, Jewish funerals do not permit cremation or embalming (except in the Reform movement), and they use coffins that are made entirely of wood. Most funerals take place within a day or two of death. The body is carefully washed and dressed in plain linen garments by a special group called the *Hevra Kadisha*, meaning "the holy society" because of the special nature of their responsibility.

Following the funeral, the family returns home for *shiva*. The word shiva means "seven" and refers to the first seven days following the funeral. During this time, mourners are prohibited from excessive grooming and pampering of the body, such as taking long baths, shaving, or trimming nails. In addition, it is customary to cover the mirrors in a shiva home. The reason for these customs is to allow the mourners to focus on their grief, instead of having to spend time worrying about their physical appearance. Mourners also do not go out of their homes during shiva; rather, the community comes in to comfort them by bringing them meals and leading services so the mourners can recite the *Kaddish*.

The mourner's kaddish is one of the most famous Jewish prayers. It is recited by mourners at the funeral, during shiva, and then for up to a year following the death. It is also recited on a *Yahrtzeit*, the anniversary of a death according to the Hebrew calendar. Interestingly, it does not mention death. Rather, it is a prayer affirming one's belief in God even after experiencing the tragedy of a loved one's death.

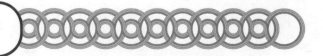

The Synagogue

The Jewish house of worship is called a *Synagogue.* Many Reform synagogues (and some others) are also called temples. In addition to being a place where Jews gather to worship, the synagogue also serves as a community and education center. The main services each week are Friday night (especially at Reform Temples) and Saturday morning, although many synagogues have services every morning and evening.

The rabbi is the religious leader and teacher of a congregation and usually speaks about the weekly Torah portion during Sabbath services. Services are usually led by a cantor who leads the singing or chanting of prayers and reads from the Torah scroll. However, anyone who is familiar with the prayers and the melodies may lead a service or read from the Torah.

In the center of the *bimah* (raised platform) at the front of the sanctuary is the *aron kodesh* (holy ark), holding the Torah scrolls. Each Torah is handwritten in Hebrew on parchment (animal skin). Above the aron is the *ner tamid* (eternal light) representing the constant presence of God and reminding us of the *menorah*, the seven-branched candle holder that illuminated the Temple in Jerusalem. There is also a podium, from which the rabbi speaks, and a table, at which the cantor sings and the Torah is read.

Below is an illustration of a common synagogue and a list of features. Locate the features in the illustration.

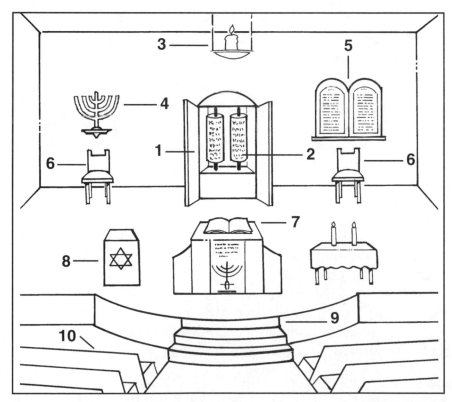

A. Congregation seating
B. Torah Scrolls
C. Ten Commandments

D. Menorah
E. Rabbi's and Cantor's seats
F. Bimah

G. Ner Tamid
H. Ark
I. Rabbi's podium
J. Cantor's and Torah reading table

Objects and Symbols

• Tallit •

A *tallit* is a four-cornered garment that is worn during the morning prayers. The important part of a tallit is the *tzitzit*, or fringes, tied onto each of the corners. The commandment to attach tzitzit to the corners of clothing comes from the Shema. The three paragraphs of the Shema contain the most important statement of belief in Judaism. Here is a portion of the third paragraph of the Shema, Numbers 15:37-41:

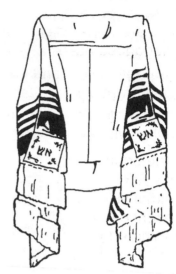

The Lord said to Moses: "Instruct the people Israel that in every generation they shall put fringes on the corners of their garments . . . . Looking upon the fringes, you will be reminded of all the commandments of the Lord and fulfill them and not be seduced by your heart or led astray by your eyes. Then you will remember and observe all My commandments and be holy before your God . . . ."

Some Jews wear a small four cornered undershirt, called a tallit katan (small tallit), so they can fulfill the commandment of wearing tzitzit all day.

• Tefillin •

Tefillin (called *phylacteries* in English) are small leather boxes with straps that can be tied on the arm and around the head. They contain verses on parchment from four sections of the Torah, including the first two paragraphs of the Shema. Tefillin are worn during morning prayers, except on Shabbat and Festivals. Wearing tefillin is a reminder of God's commandments. The tefillin on the arm (see illustration for two wrap methods) represents the opportunity to serve God with the body through doing commandments, and the tefillin on the head represents the opportunity to serve God with the mind through study and belief. The first paragraph of the Shema (Deuteronomy 6:4-9) is as follows (the commandment to wear tefillin is underlined):

Ashkenazim Wrap

Sephardim Wrap

Hear O Israel, the Lord our God, the Lord is One. You shall love the Lord your God with all your heart, with all your soul, and with all your might. These words which I command you this day shall be in your heart. You shall teach them diligently to your children. You shall recite them at home and away, morning and night. <u>You shall bind them as a sign upon your hand, they shall be a reminder above your eyes</u>, and you shall inscribe them upon the doorposts of your home and upon your gates.

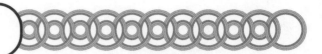

Objects and Symbols

Mezuzah

A *mezuzah* is attached to the right side of the doorpost as you enter a room. Many Jews only put a mezuzah on the front doorway, but some Jews put one on every room of the house (except closets and bathrooms), in accordance with Deuteronomy 6:9 (see the first paragraph of the Shema on page 35). Inscribed on a small piece of parchment inside the mezuzah case are the first two paragraphs of the Shema.

Kippah

A *kippah*, sometimes called a yarmelka (Yiddish) or a skullcap, is a small round cap worn on the head. The kippah is worn by men and women, although in Orthodox synagogues it is only worn by men. Some Jews wear the kippah all day; some wear it only while eating, praying, or studying; some wear it only during prayer; and some Jews (in Reform synagogues) do not wear one at all. It signifies that human beings are beneath, or dependent upon, God.

Shofar

The *shofar* is a ram's horn blown during the month prior to Rosh Hashanah (the New Year) as well as during Rosh Hashanah services and at the end of Yom Kippur (the Day of Atonement) services. Rosh Hashanah and Yom Kippur, also known as the High Holidays or the Days of Awe because of their importance, are times during which each person is judged by God. The purpose of the loud sounds of the shofar is to wake people up and remind them of their responsibility to ask forgiveness for their sins. If a person hurts another person, the first person must ask the second person for forgiveness before God will forgive him or her. If a person has committed a sin against God, then he or she may ask God directly for forgiveness.

Star of David

The six-pointed star, called a *Magen David* (shield of David) is a relatively new symbol of Judaism, becoming popular only in the last 200 years. It is named after King David, whom legend tells us had a shield with this star on it. A Magen David appears on Israel's flag.

The Jewish Calendar

Unlike the Solar Calendar, which is based on the length of time it takes the earth to circle the sun, the Jewish calendar is a lunar calendar. Every month begins with the appearance of a new moon, called *Rosh Hodesh* (the beginning of a month). A month is either 29 or 30 days long. The 12-month lunar year is about 12 days shorter than the solar year. Therefore, every two or three years the Jewish calendar adds a "leap month," an extra month to adjust the calendar so the holidays continue to fall in the proper season. The Jewish counting of years is based on the number of years since creation according to the Tanakh. Each day on the Jewish calendar begins at sundown.

JEWISH MONTHS

Tishri (Sept./Oct.)	**Heshvan** (Oct./Nov.)	**Kislev** (Nov./Dec.)	**Tevet** (Dec./Jan.)
Shebat (Jan./Feb.)	**Adar** (Feb./March)	**Nisan** (March/April)	**Iyar** (April/May)
Sivan (May/June)	**Tammuz** (June/July)	**Ab** (July/August)	**Elul** (August/Sept.)

SOME SIGNIFICANT HOLIDAYS AND THE MONTHS IN WHICH THEY FALL

Tishre: *Rosh Hashanah* (New Year), *Yom Kippur* (Day of Atonement), and *Sukkot* (the harvest Festival of Booths, a reminder of the huts in which the Israelites lived during the travels in the desert)

Kislev: *Chanukah* (the festival of the rededication of the Temple)

Adar: *Purim* (celebrating the story of Esther and the rescue of the Jews from Persia)

Nisan: *Pesach* (Passover, the Exodus from Egypt), *Yom Hashoah* (Holocaust Memorial Day), *Yom Ha'atzma'ut* (Israel Independence Day)

Sivan: *Shavuot* (festival celebrating the giving of the Torah)

Passover

PESACH

In the story of Exodus, the Israelites smeared lamb's blood on their doorposts on the night of Passover. They did this to avoid the tenth plague God sent to Pharaoh, the death of all first-born Egyptian children. Seeing the sign, God literally "passed over" their houses.

The Festival of Passover, or *Pesach,* as it is called in Hebrew, falls in the Hebrew month of Nisan (see page 37) which is late March or April. It commemorates freedom from slavery and the Exodus from Egypt. Families and friends gather to share a special meal called a *Seder* and to tell the story of Passover from a special book called a *Haggadah.* Special foods are also eaten that remind them of the hardship of slavery and the miracle of being taken out of Egypt.

At the center of a seder table is a special plate known as a seder plate, containing five (or sometimes six) items of food.

Passover Foods

Maror: a bitter herb, usually horseradish, representing the bitterness of slavery

Charoset: a mixture of apples, walnuts, cinnamon, and wine, resembling the mortar which the Israelites used to build the Egyptian cities

Z'roah: a roasted bone, often a shankbone of a lamb, representing the Passover offering

Beitzah: a roasted egg representing the new life of springtime

Karpas: a green vegetable, usually parsley, representing spring and eaten dipped in salt water, representing the tears of slavery

Hazeret: Some Seder plates have a sixth place for another bitter vegetable, usually romaine lettuce, also representing the bitterness of slavery.

You also find the following items on a Seder table:

Matzah: unleavened bread representing the bread which did not have time to rise when the Israelites left Egypt in a great hurry (Matzah also represents bread of poverty, reminding Jews of the hardship of slavery.)

Wine or grape juice: Each person drinks four cups, representing God's promise to the Jews to take them out of slavery.

PESACH (cont.)

Make a seder plate to learn about the Passover symbols. Color the plate pictured below and cut it out. Next, cut a circle the same size as the plate out of a separate sheet of paper. Then, cut along the bold lines to divide the seder plate into sections. Attach the centers of the two circles with glue or a brass fastener. (The seder plate should be on top.) Finally, lift up each section of the plate and on the paper under it write a brief description of the food that is pictured and what it symbolizes.

SEDER PLATE

Chanukah

The festival of Chanukah (also spelled Hanukkah) celebrates the defeat of the Syrian Greeks and the rededication of King Solomon's Temple by the Maccabees in 165 BCE.

The Syrians, ruled by King Antiochus, tried to force the Jews to worship the Greek Gods. He forbad them, under penalty of death, to keep the Sabbath or celebrate any Jewish holidays, circumcise their sons, or keep any other traditions of Judaism. He desecrated the Temple by placing statues of Greek gods in it, and he ordered the people to bring sacrifices of non-kosher pigs. King Antiochus sent inspectors to every town to make sure that the people carried out his instructions. The inspectors burned Torah scrolls and put to death anyone who violated the King's orders.

Menorah

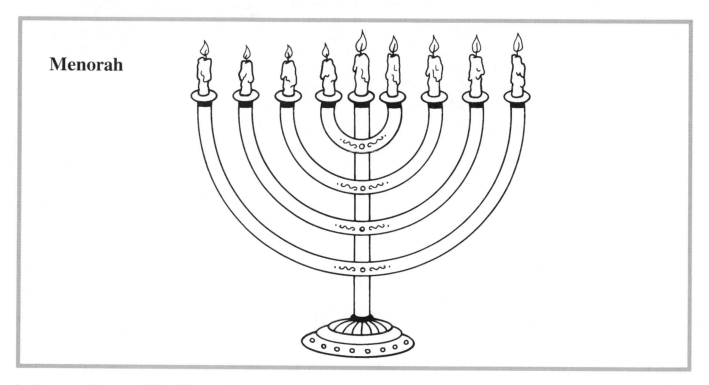

In the small town of Modi'in, a priest named Mattityahu (Mattathias) and his four sons refused to obey the king's orders. They fled to the hills and called for others to join them in fighting the Syrians. When Mattityahu died, the rebellion continued under the leadership of his son Judah, who had been given the name *Maccabee*, a Hebrew word meaning "hammer," because of his strength. Although Judah Maccabee and his followers were poorly equipped and outnumbered, they defeated the Syrian armies and recaptured all of Jerusalem.

The Temple was cleansed of idols and rededicated with feasting and great joy. A tiny container of oil was found in the Temple, enough to last one day. Miraculously, it burned for eight days and nights. That is why a special eight-branched *menorah* (candle holder) called a *chanukiyah* is lit during Chanukah, and that is also why Chanukah is sometimes called "The Festival of Lights." The ninth candle, called the *shamash*, is used to light each of the other candles. One candle is lit on the first evening, two on the second, three on the third, and so on until all eight candles are lit on the last night.

In addition to the lighting of the chanukiyah, children receive gifts and play a spinning-top game called the *dreidel* game. See the next page to make your own dreidel.

Chanukah

Making a Dreidel

1. Cut out the dreidel along the bold lines.
2. Fold along the fine inner lines and glue or tape them together so you have a box shape.
3. Make two small holes where the circles are on the top and bottom and push a short pencil through. Spin the dreidel by twirling the pencil.

Playing the Dreidel Game

A dreidel is a four-sided top. Each side has a Hebrew letter on it: *nun*, *gimmel*, *hay*, and *shin*. These four letters stand for the Hebrew words that mean "a great miracle happened there (in Israel)."

The players sit in a circle. Each player receives an equal number of tokens (nuts, candies, or coins) and puts five tokens from his or her pile into the center. Everyone takes turns spinning the dreidel. The letter on top when the dreidel stops spinning tells what to do. Players who lose their tokens are out. The last player with tokens is the winner.

> **nun:** Do nothing.
>
> **gimmel:** Take the center pile.
>
> **hay:** Take half of the center pile.
>
> **shin:** Place half of your tokens in the center pile.

Dreidel Pattern

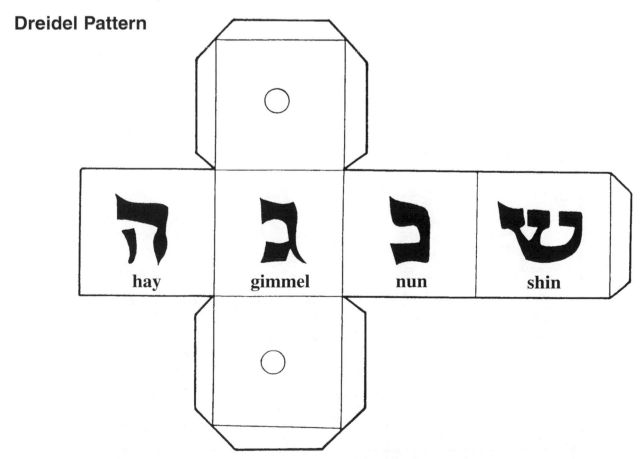

Chanukah

One traditional Jewish food is called latkes. Latkes are crispy, brown potato pancakes enjoyed on Chanukah and all year. Some people also celebrate Chanukah by eating jelly doughnuts. Both of these holiday treats are fried in oil. Remembering the story of Chanukah, why would it be important for the food to be fried in oil?

Here is a recipe for latkes. Be sure to use caution when cooking with hot oil.

Latkes

Ingredients

- 4 large potatoes
- 1 teaspoon (5 mL) salt
- 2 eggs
- 3 tablespoons (45 mL) flour
- $\frac{1}{2}$ teaspoon (3 mL) baking powder
- vegetable oil for frying
- applesauce or sour cream

Utensils

- potato peeler
- grater
- paper towels
- hand beater
- skillet
- bowl
- spoon
- spatula
- plates and forks

Preparation

1. Wash, peel, and grate the potatoes. Drain off the liquid.
2. Beat the eggs.
3. Mix everything together, except the oil.
4. Heat the oil in a skillet.
5. Drop the mixture by tablespoons into the hot oil.
6. Fry the latkes on both sides until brown.
7. Drain the latkes on paper towels.
8. Serve the latkes with applesauce or sour cream on the side.

Vocabulary Review

Place the appropriate letters in the blanks to match the vocabulary words.

_____	1. synagogue	a. wise saying
_____	2. menorah	b. the founding father of Judaism
_____	3. BCE	c. small cap worn by Jews
_____	4. Tanakh	d. before the Common Era
_____	5. polytheism	e. rite of passage for 12-year-old girls
_____	6. Passover	f. four-sided top
_____	7. shofar	g. first five books of the Hebrew Bible
_____	8. mezuzah	h. king of Egypt
_____	9. Holocaust	i. potato pancake
_____	10. pharaoh	j. eight-branched candlestick
_____	11. proverb	k. worshipping an image or idol
_____	12. monotheism	l. Common Era
_____	13. CE	m. belief in more than one god
_____	14. Moses	n. place where Jews worship
_____	15. bat mitzvah	o. symbol of the Jewish religion
_____	16. patriarch	p. murder of Jews by Nazis
_____	17. latkes	q. spiritual leader of a congregation
_____	18. idolatry	r. belief in one God
_____	19. Torah	s. prophet who lead the Exodus
_____	20. dreidel	t. ram's horn
_____	21. Star (or Shield) of David	u. holiday commemorating the Exodus
_____	22. Abraham	v. father of a tribe or nation
_____	23. rabbi	w. case attached to the doorpost of homes
_____	24. kippah	x. Hebrew Bible

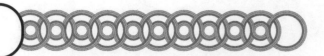

Quiz and Review

Part One: In statements 1–12, fill in the spaces with the correct answer.

1. Jews believe that God made a _____ , or sacred agreement, with Abraham.

2. The Jewish Sabbath takes place from _____ night just before sundown to _____ night after dark.

3. The Exodus took place around _____ BCE.

4. God first spoke to Moses on Mount _____ .

5. It took 10 _____ before Pharoah let the Hebrews go.

6. _____ wrote most of the Proverbs.

7. Two foods eaten on Passover are _____ and _____ .

8. Chanukah celebrates the Maccabee victory over the _____ .

9. Jews were imprisoned in _____ during the Holocaust.

10. "Bar Mitzvah" means _____ .

11. Two countries bordering Israel are _____ and _____ .

12. The _____ first destroyed King Solomon's Temple.

Part Two: Respond to the following questions in full sentences. Be sure to use details to support your answers.

1. Summarize in your own words what is at the heart of the Ten Commandments. If you could take one guiding principle from them, what would it be?

   _____

   _____

   _____

   _____

   _____

   _____

   _____

2. Why is the Western Wall sacred to Jews? How does it capture the essence of their history and religious heritage?

   _____

   _____

   _____

   _____

   _____

   _____

   _____

   _____

   _____

   _____

   _____

   _____

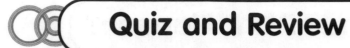

Part Two: *(cont.)*

3. Briefly explain the origin of Judaism and its basic beliefs. In what ways were the beliefs unique or new to the world?

_____

_____

_____

_____

_____

_____

_____

_____

_____

_____

_____

_____

_____

_____

_____

_____

_____

_____

_____

_____

_____

_____

_____

If you have ever read about something that happened long ago, then you are probably familiar with the abbreviations BC or BCE and AD or CE. Buddha was born in 563 BCE. Muhammad died in 632 CE. Both BC and BCE represent the years before the birth of Jesus. CE and AD mean the years after the birth of Jesus. The abbreviations stand for the following:

BC = Before Christ
AD = Anno Domini (in the year of our Lord)

BCE = Before the Common Era
CE = Common Era

In this book, only BCE and CE will be used. This is because BC and AD relate all dates to the birth of Jesus. Referring to Jesus as Christ or using dates that are based on the birth of Jesus are part of the Christian religion.

You have probably also read of events happening, for example, in the 5th century or even in the 5th century BCE. A century is 100 years. If people lived in the 1st century, they lived in the first 100 years CE, or in the first 100 years after the birth of Jesus. So, if we say something happened in the 19th century, we mean it happened during the years 1801–1900 CE. The same rule applies to the centuries BCE, only we count backwards from the birth of Jesus. For example, Buddha was born in 563 BCE, which would mean he was born in the 6th century BCE.

Here are some practice questions. You will need to use the sample time line and your math skills to find the answers.

| 2000 BCE | 1500 BCE | 1000 BCE | 500 BCE | 0 | 500 CE | 1000 CE | 1500 CE | 2000 CE |

1. Who is older, someone born in 1760 BCE or someone born in 1450 BCE?

   _____

2. How many years difference is there between 250 CE and 250 BCE?

   _____

3. How many years difference is there between 1524 CE and 1436 BCE?

   _____

4. You visit a cemetery. One of the tombstones reads: "Born in the 15th century, died in the 16th." Make up possible dates that this person may have been born and died.

   _____

5. In what century are you living now?

   _____

Page 5
1. the first five books of the Bible; Genesis, Exodus, Leviticus, Numbers, and Deuteronomy
2. The Greek Scripture tells the story of Jesus and the spread of Christianity, and is holy only to Christians, not Jews.

Page 8
1. Do not eat of the tree of knowledge of good and evil.
2. to name the creatures
3. from the rib of Adam
4. sly, clever, or crafty
5. it tempted Eve
6. to be like God
7. They loose their innocence and they feel ashamed.
8. The snake will be lowly, crawl on its stomach, and be an enemy to people. The woman will suffer in childbirth but still be desirous to mate, and she will also be subject to the man. The man will be forced to work the fields, and he will one day die.
9. to keep them from the tree of life

Page 21
1. a large group of people departed; about 1250 BCE
2. because he was drawn from the river
3. Answers will vary.
4. a. river of blood
   b. frogs
   c. lice
   d. flies
   e. death of Egyptian cattle
   f. sores
   g. hail
   h. locusts
   i. three days of darkness
   j. death of first-born children and cattle
5. They were worried about being alone. They did not trust their leader. It breaks the second commandement.
6. Ark of the Covenant; Tabernacle

Page 34
1. H	5. C	9. F
2. B	6. E	10. A
3. G	7. J	
4. D	8. I	

Page 43
1. N	9. P	17. I
2. J	10. H	18. K
3. D	11. A	19. G
4. X	12. R	20. F
5. M	13. L	21. O
6. U	14. S	22. B
7. T	15. E	23. Q
8. W	16. V	24. C

Page 44: Quiz and Review

Part One
1. covenant
2. Friday, Saturday
3. 1250 BCE
4. Sinai
5. plagues
6. King Solomon
7. (any two) matzah, beitzah (roasted egg), charoseth (an apple, nut, cinnamon and wine mixture), green vegetable, salt water, maror (bitter herb) or horseradish.
8. Syrian Greeks
9. concentration camps
10. "a son of the Commandment"
11. Jordan, Egypt, Lebanon, Syria.
12. Babylonians

Part Two
Answers will vary.

Page 47
1. 1760 BCE
2. 500 years
3. 2960 years
4. Answers will vary. One possibility is 1450-1550.
5. Through the year 2000, it is the 20th century. Beginning in 2001, it is the 21st century.